GOD IS MY
SECOND
HUSBAND

GOD IS MY SECOND HUSBAND

Published by Linda Brock, Nashville, Tennessee
Copyright © 2020 by Linda Brock

Email: Godismysecondhusband@gmail.com
Website: Godismysecondhusband.com

ISBN: 9798633747409

All scripture references are from the New International Version of the Bible.

Many thanks and much love to my daughters and their husbands: Amanda and Jason Brazier, Sarah and Tony McKay, Cynthia and Kevin Newcomb, and Laurie and Paavo Tucker. Your support and encouragement are priceless. And thank you for all the beautiful grandbabies!

Special thanks to my friends who gave me so much advice and encouragement during the writing of this book: Steve Cummings, Adeana Curry, Marty Edwards, Ray and Vessie Falconberry, Debbie Frankum, Carolyn Hughey, Laura Qualls, and Melanie Reeves.

My most profound gratitude goes to God in whom I have salvation, joy, peace, hope, and love.

CONTENTS

INTRODUCTION

The idea of God as a husband is found in the Bible. In the Old Testament, the prophet Isaiah used this symbolism to describe God's feelings for His chosen people, Israel. Rest assured: He has the same feelings for you!

> For your Maker is your husband—the LORD Almighty is his name—the Holy One of Israel is your Redeemer; he is called the God of all the earth.
>
> —Isaiah 54:5

This verse refers to ancient Israel, but we can apply it to ourselves. He, indeed, is our Redeemer.

Because of grief, loneliness, fear, or self-doubt, divorced or widowed women find themselves searching for relief from the pain. They often look for another man to fill the gaping hole in their lives, instead of allowing themselves time to grieve and process their feelings.

I am a divorced woman. As a Christian, I never thought I would have to say that. I fought for my marriage for twenty-nine years, often in brave ways and sometimes in petty ways. I finally filed for divorced after my counselor said to me: "Your husband has been cutting at the rope for years [infidelity and other things]; you just need to let go of the rope."

In some ways, the separation from my spouse was a huge relief, especially in the early days. As life progresses, I occasionally realize new sorrows. After nine years as a divorced woman, I still grieve, sometimes more than I did in the beginning.

If you are a widow, you grieve in a different way than I do. Perhaps you had a wonderful, Christian marriage. If so, I am happy for you: your relationship was rare and beautiful. Perhaps your marriage was difficult, and you feel some measure of relief from stress now that your husband is gone. Either way, you must be grieving.

If you have never been married, you may yearn for a husband. You may grieve over your singleness.

You may still be married but wonder what this book is all about. That's okay, too. But if your marriage is struggling, please, please, do everything you possibly can to heal the marriage. Of course, if you are in harm's way, please remove yourself from the situation and get to a safe place. If your husband repeatedly cheats on you, he has broken the covenant, and you can be free. Only you know your situation. Pray about it. Separate for a time if needed. Go to a counselor. Pray some more. Have friends pray for you. As in all things, pray for God's will.

God is the answer for all of us. He absorbs our grief. He is our Protector and Friend. We need to run straight to Him and find true relief, salvation, peace, and contentment. A man cannot do that for you. Only God can.

The words of Isaiah 53 have spoken to me so many times over the years. This chapter is a picture of the suffering that Jesus chose to bear for you and for me. I have used it often to center my mind during the Lord's Supper.

> He was oppressed and afflicted,
>   yet he did not open his mouth;
> he was led like a lamb to the slaughter,
>   and as a sheep before its shearers is silent,
>   so he did not open his mouth.
>
> —Isaiah 53:7

Jesus suffered for us, and His Father provided that gift. And that's just the beginning of the story of God as your Husband!

LISTEN

Open your heart, dear one, and hear
what our LORD speaks to you.

I

GOD'S LOVE
FOR YOU WILL NOT
BE SHAKEN

"Though the mountains be shaken
   and the hills be removed,
yet my unfailing love for you will not be shaken
   nor my covenant of peace be removed,"
   says the Lord, who has compassion on you.

—Isaiah 54:10

God's words to the people of Israel are a reflection of
His feelings for you today: *He loves you with an
unfailing love!*

Even when the mountains of your life are shaking and
even if the hills of your life are taken away, God's
unconditional love for you will not be shaken! You can
still have His peace. He promises you that! The Lord
God has compassion on you. He tells us:

Yet the Lord longs to be gracious to you;
   therefore he will rise up to show you compassion.
For the Lord is a God of justice.
Blessed are all who wait for him!

—Isaiah 30:18

Are the mountains upon which you built your life
shaking? Has divorce or widowhood shaken your deep
foundational beliefs?

Has the hill of your primary relationship been taken
away? Has divorce or widowhood taken away a big
part of your life? Hold tight to the unshakeable and
unchangeable God.

God's love for you will never change, no matter what you do. You don't have to be worthy of His love, and you don't have to do anything to earn it.

> . . . because God has said,
> "Never will I leave you;
>   never will I forsake you."
> So we say with confidence,
> "The Lord is my helper; I will not be afraid.
>   What can mere mortals do to me?"

—Hebrews 13:5b-6

LISTEN

God cares for you. He cares so much!
That will never change.

2

GOD INVITES YOU TO LISTEN

Listen, listen to me, and eat what is good, and
you will delight in the richest of fare. Give ear and
come to me; listen, that you may live.

—Isaiah 55:2-3a

Do you realize that God wants you to listen to Him?
He has important, life-changing things to tell you! How
must He feel when we don't listen to Him? Think
about this: How do you feel when you're eating with
people who spend most of the time looking at their
phones instead of listening to you? Did your spouse do
this to you at every meal?

Can I get a little personal here? I want to share a blog
post I wrote shortly after my divorce was final—a time
of spiritual renewal for me.

Babel, Babble, Toil, and Trouble

> *Then God blessed Noah and his sons, saying to
> them, "Be fruitful and increase in number and fill
> the earth." . . . Then they said, "Come, let us build
> ourselves a city, with a tower that reaches to the
> heavens, so that we may make a name for
> ourselves and not be scattered over the face of
> the whole earth." . . . From there the LORD
> scattered them over the face of the whole earth.*
>
> —Genesis 9:1; 11:4, 9b

*Having been born with impaired hearing, I know what
it's like to hear babble. If several people are standing
around talking, I have a difficult time hearing and
understanding what any one person is saying. I*

learned to sit close to the people that I wanted to hear, and I learned to read lips.

As a child, I loved to sit at our neighbor's kitchen table while my mom and "Aunt" Maude drank coffee and talked. My sister would be playing in another room with Aunt Maude's daughter. But I loved just listening to the conversation going on between two of my favorite people on earth. I didn't participate in the conversation; I just listened.

After the floodwaters cleansed the earth of evil men, Noah's descendants began to populate the earth. Everyone spoke the same language.

A group of men gathered together and decided to build a tower to reach the heavens. God was not part of their plan. They built the tower to build themselves up. They were not looking to raise God up. They built the tower to make a name for themselves. They were not looking to glorify the name of God. They built the tower hoping they would not be scattered over the face of the earth. They were not looking to obey God by filling the earth as He had commanded.

> *But the LORD came down to see the city and the tower that the men were building. The LORD said, "If as one people speaking the same language they have begun to do this, then nothing they plan to do will be impossible for them. Come, let us go down and confuse their language so they will not understand each other."*
>
> —*Genesis 11:5-7*

Obviously, God was not happy with the people's plan. He knew that the people were moving away from Him again. He knew they were depending on themselves once again. Their self-centeredness needed to be changed to God-centeredness. Once they stopped understanding each other, they began to understand God. It's as if God was saying, "Read My lips!"

> *So the LORD scattered them from there over all the earth, and they stopped building the city. That is why it was called Babel—because there the LORD confused the language of the whole world. From there the LORD scattered them over the face of the whole earth.*
> *—Genesis 11:8-9*

I can only imagine the confusion that ensued when the people were no longer able to communicate with each other. Babble and confusion can only be tolerated for a short while. They then had no choice but to follow God's command to populate the earth.

The people were arrogant enough to think they could build a tower tall enough to reach the heavens. We can never reach God through our own strength and will. When we try, our plans end in confusion. God wants us to humble ourselves before Him. Then He will lift us up to Him, where there is perfect peace.

This all makes me wonder if God knew what He was doing (well, of course He did!) by allowing it to be difficult for me to hear. Maybe He was protecting me from hearing things I shouldn't. Maybe by causing people's voices to sound like babble, He was encouraging me to listen to His single clear voice.

Are you listening?

We hear so much babble in the world. We need frequent times of listening to God's voice.

> Listen and hear my voice;
>   pay attention and hear what I say.

> All this also comes from the Lord Almighty,
>   whose plan is wonderful,
>   whose wisdom is magnificent.

—Isaiah 28:23, 29

LISTEN

Remove yourself from the babble and hear God's voice. It's where the richest of fare and perfect peace are found.

3

YOU WILL NOT
BE PUT TO SHAME

> "Do not be afraid; you will not be put to shame.
>   Do not fear disgrace; you will not be
> humiliated.
> You will forget the shame of your youth
>   and remember no more the reproach of your
>   widowhood."

—Isaiah 54:4

God's words to the people of Israel are a reflection of His assurance for you today: *You will forget your shame!*

No matter how you came to be alone, fear of shame and humiliation can take hold of you. Hear the words the LORD said to Joshua after Moses' death:

> "Have I not commanded you? Be strong and courageous. Do not be afraid; do not be discouraged, for the LORD your God will be with you wherever you go."

—Joshua 1:9

You may feel that you could have done something to prevent the divorce. Were you not good enough? Pretty enough? Helpful enough? Should you have stayed a few days, weeks, months, or even years longer?

You may feel that you did not do enough to prevent your husband's death. Should you have made your husband go to the doctor sooner? Did you not take care of him as well as you should have?

You may feel humiliated in your own eyes or in the eyes of others. Do you worry about what others think about you now that you are alone? Do you feel like people feel sorry for you?

LISTEN

Do not be afraid. God's got this!

4

THE LORD WILL
CALL YOU BACK

"The Lord will call you back
   as if you were a wife deserted and distressed in
spirit—
a wife who married young,
   only to be rejected," says your God.

—Isaiah 54:6

God's words to the people of Israel are a reflection of His promise to you today: *He will call you back!*

You may feel that God has abandoned you in your darkest hour, but He assures you that He is here. Take in the words spoken to David during a very painful part of his life:

The Lord is near to the brokenhearted
And saves those who are crushed in spirit.

—Psalm 34:18

Has your broken heart led you away from God? Has the pain of losing your husband crushed your spirit?

LISTEN

God is here. He is near! Hear Him calling?

5

GOD IS
YOUR REDEEMER

> . . . the Holy One of Israel is your Redeemer;
>   he is called the God of all the earth.

—Isaiah 54:5b

God's words to the people of Israel are a reflection of His offering to you today: *He is your Redeemer!*

You may feel that you cannot be forgiven for things you have done in your life. You may not feel worthy of God's grace and forgiveness. Guess what! We are all unworthy! Paul said:

> . . . for all have sinned and fall short of the glory of God, and all are justified freely by his grace through the redemption that came by Christ Jesus.

—Romans 3:23-24

If you are divorced, do you think that God's redemption is no longer for you? If you are a widow, do you think that you alone are not redeemable by God? Cry out to the Lord:

> Out of the depths I cry to you, Lord;
> Lord, hear my voice.
> Let your ears be attentive
>   to my cry for mercy.
> If you, Lord, kept a record of sins,
>   Lord, who could stand?
> But with you there is forgiveness,
>   so that we can, with reverence, serve you.
> I wait for the Lord, my whole being waits,
>   and in his word I put my hope.

I wait for the Lord
　　more than watchmen wait for the morning,
　　more than watchmen wait for the morning.
Israel, put your hope in the Lord,
　　for with the Lord is unfailing love
　　and with him is full redemption.

—Psalm 130:1-7

LISTEN

God can redeem you. Yes, you!

6

GOD IS YOUR HUSBAND

"For your Maker is your husband—
the Lord Almighty is his name..."

—Isaiah 54:5a

God's words to the people of Israel are a reflection of His covenant with you today: *He is your Husband!*

You are not alone after all. Never alone!

The word "husband" is an abbreviation for "house-band," meaning one who binds, secures, encircles, and strengthens. No one can do that for you better than God.

God Almighty made you:

For you created my inmost being;
   you knit me together in my mother's womb.
I praise you because I am fearfully and
wonderfully made;
   your works are wonderful,
   I know that full well.

—Psalm 139:13-14

God Almighty knows everything about you:

You have searched me, Lord,
   and you know me.
You know when I sit and when I rise;
   you perceive my thoughts from afar.
You discern my going out and my lying down;
   you are familiar with all my ways.

—Psalm 139:1-2

Just as marriage is intended to be a covenant between a husband and a wife, God makes a covenant with us:

> Though the mountains be shaken
>   and the hills be removed,
> yet my unfailing love for you will not be shaken
>   nor my covenant of peace be removed,"
>   says the Lord, who has compassion on you.

—Isaiah 54:10

God's Son, Jesus, ultimately established this covenant of peace at the Last Supper:

> In the same way, after the supper he took the cup, saying, "This cup is the new covenant in my blood, which is poured out for you."

—Luke 22:20

LISTEN

God wants a covenant relationship with you!

7

GOD INVITES YOU
TO THE FEAST

> Why spend money on what is not bread,
>   and your labor on what does not satisfy?
> Listen, listen to me, and eat what is good,
>   and you will delight in the richest of fare.

—Isaiah 55:2

God's words to the people of Israel are a reflection of His invitation to you today: *Come to the feast!*

What is the richest of fare? Is it expensive food? No, it is spiritual food—food that we cannot purchase with money.

> Come, all you who are thirsty,
>   come to the waters;
> and you who have no money,
>   come, buy and eat!
> Come, buy wine and milk
>   without money and without cost.

—Isaiah 55:1

We find this food when we turn to God's Word and learn about Jesus.

> Then Jesus declared, "I am the bread of life. Whoever comes to me will never go hungry, and whoever believes in me will never be thirsty.

—John 6:35

The Lord's Supper is a feast of hope that we share each Sunday. We take the bread and we drink the cup and we remember His great sacrifice. We take the bread, and in our hearts, we see His nail-scarred hands and feet. We take the cup, and in our hearts, we see

30

the lifeblood flow from His pierced side. We feel sadness, and then we feel deep gratitude. He did this so that we can be with Him in heaven one day. We will partake of the Great Banquet!

The Great Banquet is a feast of fulfillment and was prophesied in Isaiah:

> On this mountain the Lord Almighty will prepare
>   a feast of rich food for all peoples,
> a banquet of aged wine—
>   the best of meats and the finest of wines.

—Isaiah 25:6

As we partake of the Lord's Supper, we look forward to the Great Banquet in heaven. In our everyday lives, the feast is Jesus, the Bread of Life.

LISTEN

Feast on Jesus every day.

8

GOD MADE YOU
IN HIS IMAGE

And just as we have borne the image of the earthly man, so shall we bear the image of the heavenly man.

—1 Corinthians 15:49

Consider this post from my blog:

Created in the Image of God

> *So God created man in his own image, in the image of God he created him; male and female he created them.*
>
> *—Genesis 1:27*

Born at Huntsville Hospital in Huntsville, Alabama, in May of 1960, I sported a full head of dark brown hair. Cute. I had all of my fingers and toes. I looked perfect. Except for my right ear. This ear curled toward the front. Not just a little. A lot. Deformed. Imperfect.

Don't get me wrong. I think sticky outie ears—you know, the ones that curl in just a little—are cute. Some of the cutest children I've ever seen have had two little ears that stick out just a little. But my one sticky outie ear was not cute to me. Maybe because it was just the one ear that was that way. Ears are supposed to look alike. Symmetrical. Aren't they? (My parents paid for me to have plastic surgery, but I still wasn't pleased with the appearance of that ear.)

Did God make a mistake? Never. Did it take years for me to deal with having a "deformed" ear? Yes.

The dictionary defines "deformed" as having the form changed. So, according to that definition, God decided to change the form of my ear. He can do that and still love me. He can do that and still make me in His image. Because being made in God's image has nothing to do with physical appearance. It's all about the Spirit. And the fruit of the Spirit is love, joy, peace, patience, kindness, goodness, faithfulness, gentleness and self-control (Galatians 5:22-23). There's nothing in there about ears that God has decided to change from the norm.

Did God decide to change the form of anything on your body? Maybe you have a birthmark on your neck. Maybe you have eyes that are too close together. Do you have a uni-brow? Come on. Surely there's something about your body that's different from most people.

I have often thought of my creatively formed ear as my thorn in the flesh. Remember Paul's thorn? Well, we don't know exactly what that was, but you remember that he had a thorn, right?

> *Even if I should choose to boast, I would not be a fool, because I would be speaking the truth. But I refrain, so no one will think more of me than is warranted by what I do or say. To keep me from becoming conceited because of these surpassingly great revelations, there was given me a thorn in my flesh, a messenger of Satan, to torment me. Three times I pleaded with the Lord to take it away from me.*
> *—2 Corinthians 12:6-8*

We need to ask ourselves "Am I willing to accept the way God has formed my body?" God formed you the way you are for a reason. Paul told us that God gave him a thorn "to keep me from becoming conceited." Maybe that's why I have a thorny ear. Maybe that's why you have a unibrow. Maybe we look the way we do just because God has a sense of humor. I don't know. But I do know one thing: This physical body is only temporary. And some day, sooner or later, my body will be changed "in the twinkling of an eye." I like to think of the twinkling eye being God's eye when He sees me in my new and perfect heavenly body—my spiritual body—which will be filled with love, joy, peace, patience, kindness, goodness, faithfulness, gentleness and self-control. Just like our Maker.

We often focus on our physical bodies more than we should. Instead, let's focus on our spiritual bodies.

> For physical training is of some value, but godliness has value for all things, holding promise for both the present life and the life to come.
>
> —1 Timothy 4:8

LISTEN

Accept your physical body and focus on your spiritual being.

36

9

GOD GIVES YOU THE ULTIMATE DESIGNER CLOTHES

> I delight greatly in the Lord; my soul rejoices in my God. For he has clothed me with garments of salvation and arrayed me in a robe of his righteousness, as a bridegroom adorns his head like a priest, and as a bride adorns herself with her jewels.
>
> —Isaiah 61:10

Don't you just love to put on your favorite outfit? Maybe it fits you well or brings out the color of your eyes. Maybe the feel and flow of the fabric suits your personality. Maybe the garment was created by a top designer (I'm an *Umgee* girl myself). Whatever the reason, a favorite outfit can make you feel happy and can boost your confidence.

What if you could wear the ultimate designer clothes? You can! God is the Master Designer. He wants to clothe us with "garments of salvation" and array us in "a robe of His righteousness."

Paul tells us:

> So in Christ Jesus you are all children of God through faith, for all of you who were baptized into Christ have clothed yourselves with Christ.
>
> —Galatians 3:26-27

So much more than any earthly clothes, being clothed with Christ fills you with joy and raises your level of confidence to new heights!

What do we do with these new spiritual clothes? Do we wear our old sinful clothes under the new clean clothes? Do we toss them on the floor of our closets and forget about them? Do we tear them or rip them apart at the seams?

Or, do we follow the care instructions He gives us? (The care instructions aren't on a hidden tag; the Bible is our instruction manual.) The answer is obvious, but how must God feel when we don't take care of our spiritual clothes? Read these words of Paul:

> But now you must also rid yourselves of all such things as these: anger, rage, malice, slander, and filthy language from your lips. Do not lie to each other, since you have taken off your old self with its practices.
>
> —Colossians 3:8-9

Let's not rip at our spiritual clothes by acting according to the sinful nature. Instead, let's follow the care instructions that Paul gave us in the Bible:

> . . . as God's chosen people, holy and dearly loved, clothe yourselves with compassion, kindness, humility, gentleness and patience. Bear with each other and forgive one another if any of you has a grievance against someone. Forgive as the Lord forgave you. And over all these virtues put on love, which binds them all together in perfect unity.
>
> —Colossians 3:12-14

One of my favorite hymns is "Ivory Palaces," written in 1915 by Henry Barraclough. As you read these words, let the joy of your salvation wash over you, and take a moment to cherish your spiritual clothes.

> My Lord has garments so wondrous fine,
> And myrrh their texture fills;
> Its fragrance reached to this heart of mine
> With joy my being thrills.
>
> His life had also its sorrows sore,
> For aloes had a part;
> And when I think of the cross He bore,
> My eyes with teardrops start.
>
> His garments, too, were in cassia dipped,
> With healing in a touch;
> In paths of sin had my feet e'er slipped—
> He's saved me from its clutch.
>
> In garments glorious He will come,
> To open wide the door;
> And I shall enter my heav'nly home,
> To dwell forevermore.
>
> *Refrain*
> Out of the ivory palaces,
> Into a world of woe,
> Only His great eternal love
> Made my Savior go.

What precious words to remind us of the Lord's sacrifice and the cost of our spiritual clothes!

LISTEN

Christ provided you with the ultimate spiritual clothes. Take good care of them by following the instructions found in the Bible.

10

YOU ARE NOT FORGOTTEN

But Zion said, "The LORD has forsaken me,
the Lord has forgotten me."

"Can a mother forget the baby at her breast
and have no compassion on the child she has
borne? Though she may forget,
I will not forget you! See, I have engraved you on
the palms of my hands; your walls are ever
before me."

—Isaiah 49:14-16

On your wedding day, you made a commitment to
someone, meaning it with all your heart, and you
heard words like this spoken back to you: ". . . to have
and to hold from this day forward, for better, for
worse, for richer, for poorer, in sickness and in health,
to love and to cherish from this day forward until
death do us part."

Do those words now bring you anguish? Do you
sometimes feel abandoned and forgotten? Take heart,
dear one! Absorb the words God spoke to the ancient
Israelites: "I will not forget you!" These words also are
a picture of God's commitment to you.

When Moses and the Israelites left Egypt and were
wandering in the wilderness on the way to the
Promised Land, Moses reminded the people:

Know therefore that the Lord your God is God; he
is the faithful God, keeping his covenant of love
to a thousand generations of those who love him
and keep his commandments.

—Deuteronomy 7:9

44

Do you want evidence that someone special is truly committed to you? The ring on your spouse's left hand was a symbol of his commitment to you, but look at this: Jesus bears the marks of His commitment to you on both of His hands.

The perfect Jesus Christ died on the cross for you, and His nail-scarred hands are profoundly more precious than a wedding ring on a man's finger. Receive this: You are engraved on the palms of His hands. Your name, your problems, your insecurities, your desires, and everything about you are inscribed on His hands.

As your second husband, God only has to look at His Son's hands to remember His commitment to You. He does not forget you. It would be impossible. He holds you in His hands, and you are cherished and protected there.

Knowing you are indelibly written on Jesus' hands, make every attempt to override your feelings of abandonment. Cling to God's covenant promise. Celebrate His grace, serve others, and practice gratitude.

LISTEN

You are remembered, and you are loved.

II

GOD WILL HELP YOU FIND FORGIVENESS

"Come now, let us settle the matter,"
    says the Lord.
"Though your sins are like scarlet,
    they shall be as white as snow;
though they are red as crimson,
    they shall be like wool."

—Isaiah 1:18

We are all sinners. Our sins are like scarlet before God. There's just no way around that fact. You may even be at least partially responsible for the deterioration of your marriage.

> . . . for all have sinned and fall short of the glory of God.
>
> —Romans 3:23

> If we claim we have not sinned, we make him out to be a liar and his word is not in us.
>
> —1 John 1:10

By God's grace, through the death, burial, and resurrection of Jesus, we can be forgiven and have the hope of heaven. Please read or sing the words of Fanny Crosby's beautiful hymn "Though Your Sins Be as Scarlet":

> Though your sins be as scarlet,
> They shall be as white as snow;
> Though your sins be as scarlet,
> They shall be as white as snow;
> Though they be red like crimson,
> They shall be as wool!

Though your sins be as scarlet,
Though your sins be as scarlet,
They shall be as white as snow,
They shall be as white as snow.

Hear the voice that entreats you,
Oh, return ye unto God!
Hear the voice that entreats you,
Oh, return ye unto God!
He is of great compassion,
And of wondrous love;
Hear the voice that entreats you,
Hear the voice that entreats you,
Oh, return ye unto God!
Oh, return ye unto God!

He'll forgive your transgressions,
And remember them no more;
He'll forgive your transgressions,
And remember them no more;
"Look unto Me, ye people,"
Saith the Lord your God!
He'll forgive your transgressions,
He'll forgive your transgressions,
And remember them no more,
And remember them no more.

This song reminds us that we should be so grateful for our salvation. Here are other reminders of what He has done for us:

If we confess our sins, he is faithful and just and will forgive us our sins and purify us from all unrighteousness.

—1 John 1:9

He has not punished us as we deserve for all our sins, for his mercy toward those who fear and honor him is as great as the height of the heavens above the earth.

—Psalm 103:10-14

. . . because of the surpassing grace God has given you. Thanks be to God for his indescribable gift!

—2 Corinthians 9:14b-15

Dear one, I'm reminding you of God's forgiveness of your sins, because He asks you to forgive those who have wronged you. Once we are able to accept that we need God's forgiveness, we are on our way to truly being able to forgive others. God knows that we need to be released from resentment before we can have true joy and be a light to others.

And do not grieve the Holy Spirit of God, with whom you were sealed for the day of redemption. Get rid of all bitterness, rage and anger, brawling and slander, along with every form of malice. Be kind and compassionate to one another, forgiving each other, just as in Christ God forgave you.

—Ephesians 4:30-32

Forgiveness doesn't mean that you should deny reality, and it doesn't mean that you should go back to being a victim of unfaithfulness and abuse. Forgiveness is for your peace of mind.

Do you harbor indignation and bitterness against your ex-spouse? Do you feel like your spirit has been mortally wounded? I am so sorry! I know firsthand the pain of rejection and betrayal, and I beg you to ask God to help you release the anger you feel. If you don't let go of the bitterness, rage, and anger, you will grieve the Holy Spirit.

As a widow, you may feel anger and resentment because your husband left you all alone. You may be overwhelmed with life because your husband left you to take care of so many things that he used to do for you and your family.

As a single person, you may resent God for not providing you with a spouse. Or you may be angry with a certain man who disappointed.

You cannot forgive on your own. But over time, with God's help, you can forgive.

> Therefore, as God's chosen people, holy and dearly loved, clothe yourselves with compassion, kindness, humility, gentleness and patience. Bear with each other and forgive one another if any of you has a grievance against someone. Forgive as the Lord forgave you.
>
> —Colossians 3:12-13

As you continually seek knowledge from God's Word, courage through prayer, and strength from the Holy Spirit, you will find forgiveness for your ex-spouse. Truthfully, forgiveness can be a mental decision before it becomes an emotional reality.

Set your minds on things above, not on earthly things.

—Colossians 3:2

After you make the decision to forgive, take the time to make sure your forgiveness is indeed an emotional reality. Without that, resentment will fester, and it will steal your joy. Please don't let your ex-spouse do that to you. Choose forgiveness. Choose life.

LISTEN

God loved you so much that He gave His only Son to die on a cross to make it possible for God to forgive your sins. Dear one, accept His forgiveness and please share it!

12

THE HOLY SPIRIT WILL FILL YOUR EMPTINESS

I pray that out of his glorious riches he may strengthen you with power through his Spirit in your inner being, so that Christ may dwell in your hearts through faith. And I pray that you, being rooted and established in love, may have power, together with all the Lord's holy people, to grasp how wide and long and high and deep is the love of Christ, and to know this love that surpasses knowledge—that you may be filled to the measure of all the fullness of God.

—Ephesians 3:16-19

Paul's earnest prayer written to the Ephesians is also my wholehearted prayer for you.

My dad was a kind and humble Christian man. During the last phase of his battle with multiple myeloma, he was in so much pain, but he never complained. I took him to the doctor one day, and the news was not good. On the way home, he suggested that we stop for lunch. After we got back in the car, I asked him if his lunch was good. He said something that I'll never forget: "It filled a hole."

Has your divorce or the death of your spouse left a gaping hole in your soul? Please ask God to fill it and then watch Him work in your life.

May the God of hope fill you with all joy and peace as you trust in him, so that you may overflow with hope by the power of the Holy Spirit.

—Romans 15:13

So then, just as you received Christ Jesus as Lord, continue to live your lives in him, rooted and built up in him, strengthened in the faith as you were taught, and overflowing with thankfulness. See to it that no one takes you captive through hollow and deceptive philosophy, which depends on human tradition and the elemental spiritual forces of this world rather than on Christ. For in Christ all the fullness of the Deity lives in bodily form.

—Colossians 2:6-9

LISTEN

Let the Holy Spirit fill your emptiness
and then use it for His glory.

13

GOD WANTS TO
ENGAGE YOU

Whoever acknowledges me before others, I will also acknowledge before my Father in heaven.

—Matthew 10:32

Dear one, if you aren't a Christian, you may be wondering how to go about becoming a Christ follower and receiving the Holy Spirit. At some point, we must all face our lostness:

. . . for all have sinned and fall short of the glory of God.

—Romans 3:23

For the wages of sin is death, but the gift of God is eternal life in Christ Jesus our Lord.

—Romans 6:23

The good news—the Gospel—is that God provided a way of escape from our sinfulness:

For God so loved the world that he gave his one and only Son, that whoever believes in him shall not perish but have eternal life.

—John 3:16

Our way of escape is Jesus Christ, who was sent by Father God to die on the old rugged cross and then was resurrected to new life—a symbol of the new life you can have in Him.

Take in the words of George Bennard's hymn "The Old Rugged Cross":

58

On a hill far away stood an old rugged cross,
  The emblem of suff'ring and shame,
And I love that old cross where the Dearest and Best
  For a world of lost sinners was slain.

So I'll cherish the old rugged cross,
  Till my trophies at last I lay down;
I will cling to the old rugged cross,
  And exchange it some day for a crown.

Oh, that old rugged cross, so despised by the world,
  Has a wondrous attraction for me;
For the dear Lamb of God left His glory above,
  To bear it to dark Calvary.

In the old rugged cross, stained with blood so divine,
  A wondrous beauty I see;
For 'twas on that old cross Jesus suffered and died,
  To pardon and sanctify me.

Those words deeply and profoundly impact me. I pray they do you as well.

You may be asking: What does God want me to do? How can I be pardoned and sanctified?

God asks us to hear His message:

> Consequently, faith comes from hearing the message, and the message is heard through the word about Christ.

> —Romans 10:17

And you also were included in Christ when you heard the message of truth, the gospel of your salvation.

—Ephesians 1:13a

As we read God's Word, we are hearing what God asks of us. We can't receive salvation until we hear what God requires. Once we hear it, we must believe it.

And without faith it is impossible to please God, because anyone who comes to him must believe that he exists and that he rewards those who earnestly seek him.

—Hebrews 11:6

Jesus said to His followers:

I told you that you would die in your sins; if you do not believe that I am he, you will indeed die in your sins.

—John 8:24

The book of John was written so that we would believe:

Jesus performed many other signs in the presence of his disciples, which are not recorded in this book. But these are written that you may believe that Jesus is the Messiah, the Son of God, and that by believing you may have life in his name.

—John 20:31

When you truly believe in someone, do you ignore him, or do you act on that belief? When we hear about Jesus and believe that He is God's Son, we want to follow what He says. God asks that we turn away from sin and follow His path to life. To do this, we confess our sins and turn away from them.

> Whoever conceals their sins does not prosper, but the one who confesses and renounces them finds mercy.
>
> —Proverbs 28:13

> . . . now he commands all people everywhere to repent.
>
> —Acts 17:30

Read the words of the writer of 2 Corinthians:

> Even if I caused you sorrow by my letter, I do not regret it. Though I did regret it—I see that my letter hurt you, but only for a little while—yet now I am happy, not because you were made sorry, but because your sorrow led you to repentance. For you became sorrowful as God intended and so were not harmed in any way by us. Godly sorrow brings repentance that leads to salvation and leaves no regret, but worldly sorrow brings death.
>
> —2 Corinthians 7:8-10

Only through bringing about a sense of sorrow for our sins can we come to true repentance.

True belief in Jesus and repentance of our sins lead us to acknowledge Him to others.

> For it is with your heart that you believe and are justified, and it is with your mouth that you profess your faith and are saved.
>
> —Romans 10:10

We can think of our blossoming understanding and faith, which brings about repentance from sin and confession of Christ as the Son of God, as an engagement. In the next chapter, we'll talk about the defining moment of salvation: baptism, a symbolic and transforming event.

LISTEN

God is tenderly calling you!

14

GOD CAN SAVE
YOUR SOUL

Peter replied, "Repent and be baptized, every one of you, in the name of Jesus Christ for the forgiveness of your sins. And you will receive the gift of the Holy Spirit."

—Acts 2:38

Baptism is a beautiful act of submission. Through baptism, we participate in the story of Jesus Christ, who died on a cross, was buried, and rose again:

For Christ also suffered once for sins, the righteous for the unrighteous, to bring you to God. He was put to death in the body but made alive in the Spirit.

—1 Peter 3:18

When we are submersed in water, our old sinful self is put to death. When we are brought up out of the water, we are made alive in the Spirit, ready to live a new life. What beautiful symbolism. The power is not in the water; it's in the resurrection of Jesus.

. . . not the removal of dirt from the body but the pledge of a clear conscience toward God. It saves you by the resurrection of Jesus Christ.

—1 Peter 1:21b

Baptism saves us, but it must be done in honest faith in the power of the cross. Paul told the Galatians:

So in Christ Jesus you are all children of God through faith, for all of you who were baptized into Christ have clothed yourselves with Christ.

—Galatians 3:26-27

A wonderful summary of baptism is found in Romans:

> What shall we say, then? Shall we go on sinning so that grace may increase? By no means! We are those who have died to sin; how can we live in it any longer? Or don't you know that all of us who were baptized into Christ Jesus were baptized into his death? We were therefore buried with him through baptism into death in order that, just as Christ was raised from the dead through the glory of the Father, we too may live a new life.
>
> —Romans 6:1-4

Baptism is like a beautiful wedding ceremony. You commit yourself wholeheartedly to God, and He promises to save you. He indwells you with the Holy Spirit, a seal of the commitment between you. This seal is symbolic of a wedding ring. You even get a new name and identity: Christian, a new creation.

LISTEN

Will you surrender your life and will to God?

15

GOD GIVES YOU
A NEW IDENTITY

"Forget the former things;
   do not dwell on the past.
See, I am doing a new thing!
   Now it springs up; do you not perceive it?"

—Isaiah 43:18-19

As Christians, we can put the past behind us and look forward to a new life—one that God provides. Life may not be easy all of the time, but we have the assurance that God is with us every step of the way.

And surely I am with you always, to the very end of the age.

—Matthew 28:20b

When times get tough, we can look back at our baptism, the point when we accepted God's grace, and remember His commitment to us. We remember the love, faith, and support that we felt during the ceremony, and we use that as our anchor. Our baptism is a tangible reminder of God's sacrifice and our coming reward. It helps us remember that He is our Redeemer and Friend.

When we are completely united with Christ, we no longer identify as lonely, scared, restless, and unhappy. We may sometimes feel these things, but in Christ, we find fellowship with other believers, courage to conquer every fear, peace that passes understanding, and joy beyond measure.

God is love, and our new identity is love. The following is one of the best-known scriptures in the Bible:

Love is patient, love is kind. It does not envy, it
does not boast, it is not proud. It does not
dishonor others, it is not self-seeking, it is not
easily angered, it keeps no record of wrongs.
Love does not delight in evil but rejoices with the
truth. It always protects, always trusts, always
hopes, always perseveres. Love never fails.

—1 Corinthians 13:4-8a

Dear one, this identity may look impossible to you, but
every moment is a fresh start, and God promises to
help you.

I lift up my eyes to the mountains—
    where does my help come from?
My help comes from the Lord,
    the Maker of heaven and earth.

—Psalm 121:1-2

I can do all this through him who gives me
strength.

—Philippians 4:13

Even when we fail and even when things don't seem
to make sense, God is working everything out for our
ultimate good.

And we know that in all things God works for the
good of those who love him, who have been
called according to his purpose.

—Romans 8:28

God is with you for better or for worse, and even
death will not separate you.

For I am convinced that neither death nor life, neither angels nor demons, neither the present nor the future, nor any powers, neither height nor depth, nor anything else in all creation, will be able to separate us from the love of God that is in Christ Jesus our Lord.

—Romans 8:38-39

LISTEN

Your new identity is love!

16

GOD IS STILL WRITING YOUR STORY

Strengthen the feeble hands,
    steady the knees that give way;
say to those with fearful hearts,
    "Be strong, do not fear;
your God will come,
    he will come with vengeance;
with divine retribution
    he will come to save you."

—Isaiah 35:3-4

Have you ever read a novel with lots of descriptions of the characters and lots of seemingly disconnected scenes? Did you feel like you would never be able to understand what was going on? As you continued to read, everything started to fall into place. All of the different characters and scenes became connected, and the confusion, intrigue, and mystery were totally worth the outcome.

Sometimes, our lives are like that kind of book. We go through difficulties, sometimes one piled on top of another, and we wonder how we'll ever make sense of what's happening to us. We need to remember that God hasn't finished writing our stories.

You are like a diamond that is beautiful because of the pressure and heat that it has undergone. God takes you, a diamond in the rough, and through trials, difficulties, and life experiences, shapes you into something stunning.

Like a loving husband, God wants to help you through your trials and difficulties. He wants to hold your hand and assure you that everything will turn out for your good. God knows that time is fleeting:

But do not forget this one thing, dear friends:
With the Lord a day is like a thousand years, and
a thousand years are like a day.

—2 Peter 3:8

God can use the difficulties in your life to make you a more grateful person, to use you as an example for others, and to give you a new confidence in His provision and care.

God says the following to the people of Israel, but we can broaden the application to include ourselves:

Behold, I have refined you, but not as silver;
 I have tested you in the furnace of affliction.
For my own sake, for my own sake, I do this.
 How can I let myself be defamed?
 I will not yield my glory to another.

—Isaiah 48:10-11

Not only are we made stronger through trials, but God can use our trials to glorify His holy name.

When you allow Him to show up in your story, He will restore you and heal you. He is the Great Physician, and in the end, He will make all things new.

Then I saw a new heaven and a new earth, for the first heaven and the first earth had passed away, and the sea was no more. And I saw the holy city, new Jerusalem, coming down out of heaven from God, prepared as a bride adorned for her husband. And I heard a loud voice from the throne saying, "Behold, the dwelling place of

God is with man. He will dwell with them, and they will be his people, and God himself will be with them as their God. He will wipe away every tear from their eyes, and death shall be no more, neither shall there be mourning, nor crying, nor pain anymore, for the former things have passed away."

And he who was seated on the throne said, "Behold, I am making all things new." Also he said, "Write this down, for these words are trustworthy and true." And he said to me, "It is done! I am the Alpha and the Omega, the beginning and the end. To the thirsty I will give from the spring of the water of life without payment.

—Revelation 21:1-6

This picture of heaven makes me long for our eternal home. I want to live my life story in such a way that when the end comes, I will joyfully skip to Him and wrap my arms tightly around His precious neck.

LISTEN

You are a diamond in God's eyes!

Made in the USA
Coppell, TX
16 April 2020